SOLE SURVIVOR

SURVIVING THE SEA

Louise Spilsbury

Please visit our website, www.garethstevens.com.
For a free color catalog of all our high-quality books,
call toll free 1-800-542-2595 or fax 1-877-542-2596.

CATALOGING-IN-PUBLICATION DATA

Names: Spilsbury, Louise.
Title: Surviving the sea / Louise Spilsbury.
Description: New York : Gareth Stevens Publishing, 2017. | Series: Sole survivor | Includes index.
Identifiers: ISBN 9781482450712 (pbk.) | ISBN 9781482450736 (library bound) | ISBN 9781482450729 (6 pack)
Subjects: LCSH: Survival at sea--Juvenile literature.
Classification: LCC GF86.S65 2017 | DDC 910.4'52--dc23

First Edition

Published in 2017 by
Gareth Stevens Publishing
111 East 14th Street, Suite 349
New York, NY 10003

© 2017 Gareth Stevens Publishing

Produced for Gareth Stevens by Calcium
Editors: Sarah Eason and Jennifer Sanderson
Designer: Paul Myerscough

Picture credits: Cover: Shutterstock: Willyam Bradberry (right), Dudarev Mikhail (left). Inside: Shutterstock: Haider Y. Abdulla 34–35, Matusciac Alexandru 39, Pierre-Yves Babelon 36–37, Darren Baker 42–43, Bierchen 30–31, Bildagentur Zoonar GmbH 37, Blend Images 9, Bonevoyage 20–21, Rich Carey 22–23, 24–25, 27, CURA Photography 12–13, Elsa Hoffmann 1, 28–29, Irabel8 6–7, Brian A Jackson 18–19, Iakov Kalinin 14–15, Laura D 26–27, Carsten Medom Madsen 41, Dudarev Mikhail 16–17, Redchanka 4–5, Russal 8–9, Samot 32–33, Eugene Sergeev 43, Sutiporn 22, Vibrant Image Studio 38–39, Krivosheev Vitaly 35, Maksim Vivtsaruk 33, Weintel 40–41, Richard Whitcombe 5, David Wingate 10–11, Dmytro Zinkevych 18.

All rights reserved. No part of this book may be reproduced in any form without permission from the publisher, except by reviewer.

Printed in the United States of America
CPSIA compliance information: Batch #CS16GS:
For further information contact Gareth Stevens, New York, New York at 1-800-542-2595.

CONTENTS

Chapter One Sea Dangers — 4
Capsized! — 6
Staying Afloat — 8
Life Raft — 10

Chapter Two Exposed — 12
Chilled to the Bone — 14
Surviving the Sun — 16

Chapter Three Food and Drink — 18
Drinking Water — 20
Catching Fish — 22
Other Foods — 24

Chapter Four Under Attack! — 26
Sharks — 28
Jellyfish — 30
Pirates! — 32

Chapter Five Navigation — 34
Risky Landings — 36
Stranded! — 38

Chapter Six Rescue! — 40
Be Prepared — 42

Answers — 44
Glossary — 46
For More Information — 47
Index — 48

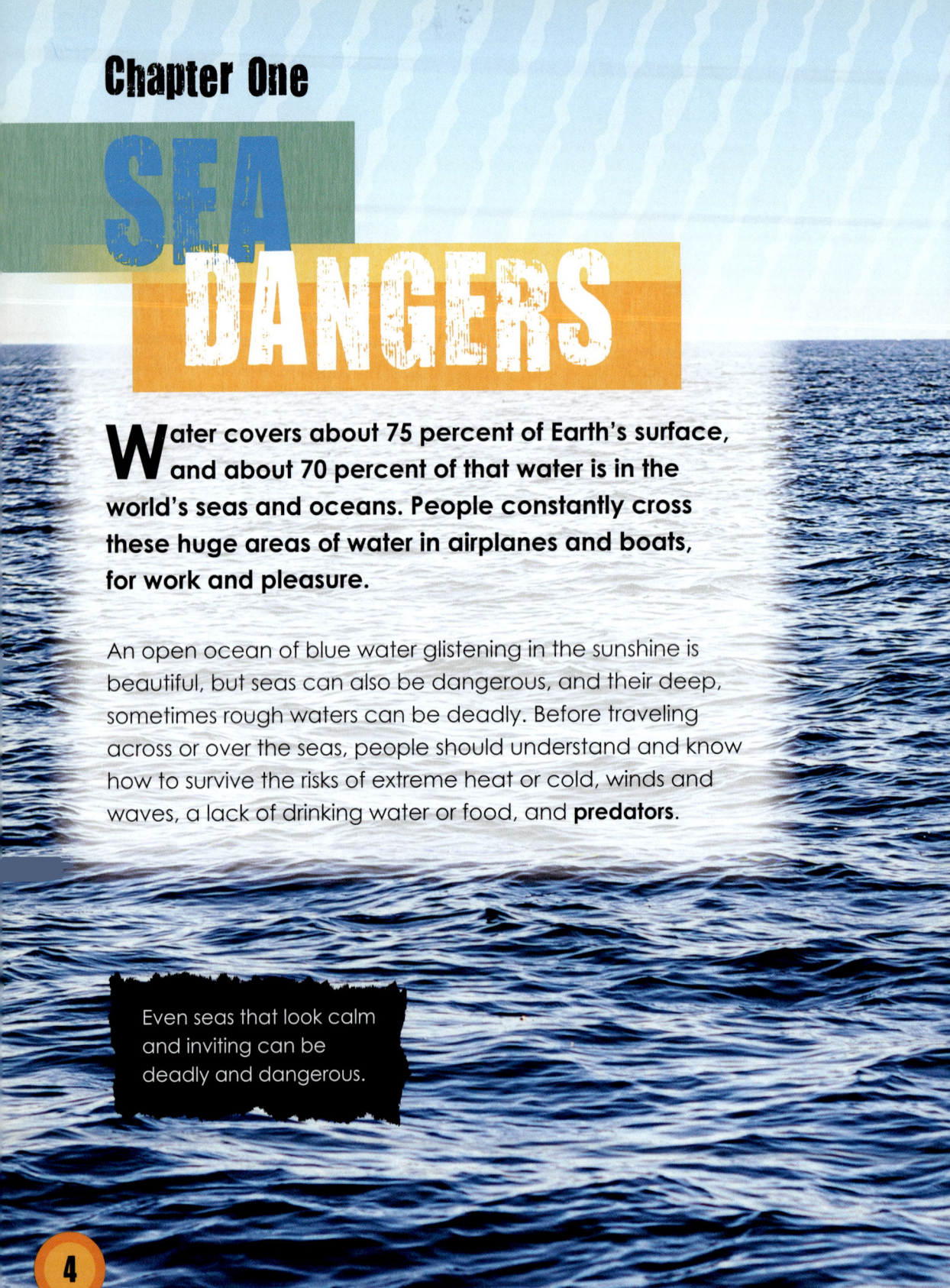

Chapter One
SEA DANGERS

Water covers about 75 percent of Earth's surface, and about 70 percent of that water is in the world's seas and oceans. People constantly cross these huge areas of water in airplanes and boats, for work and pleasure.

An open ocean of blue water glistening in the sunshine is beautiful, but seas can also be dangerous, and their deep, sometimes rough waters can be deadly. Before traveling across or over the seas, people should understand and know how to survive the risks of extreme heat or cold, winds and waves, a lack of drinking water or food, and **predators**.

Even seas that look calm and inviting can be deadly and dangerous.

Airplane Down!

Most airplanes cross oceans without a hitch. Once in a while, an aircraft has engine trouble and crash-lands in the sea. In order to survive until rescuers arrive, people should do the following:

- Get to a life raft.
- Swim clear of the aircraft, or row away from it if in a raft.
- Stay nearby because the airplane may be sending distress signals to help rescuers find it.
- Move away from any fuel-covered water in case it catches fire.
- Try to find other survivors.
- Keep calm. Airplanes follow set routes and rescuers should be on their way.

In this book, we are going to look at some of the hazards people face in seas, and how some people have survived the most terrifying dangers of all.

Passengers often escape a crash-landing at sea, but the airplanes they flew in may remain wrecked at the bottom of the sea.

Read each page carefully—there are a lot of survival tips and some great information that will help you correctly answer the Do or Die questions. You can find the answers on pages 44 and 45.

CAPSIZED!

Boats are designed to cope with being blasted by winds and tossed by most waves. Wind creates waves because when it blow over the sea, it transfers some of its energy to the water through **friction** between the air and the water. Stronger winds cause larger waves, and these can **capsize** boats. Boats also capsize and sink if they hit rocks.

Stormy weather can push boats against rocks, damaging and capsizing them.

As boats capsize, anything inside that is not tied down is tossed around. People have to hold on tight to keep themselves from being thrown against the sides of the boat. If lucky, they may be able to pull the boat back into an upright position or plug a hole made by a rock so they can keep going.

"I SURVIVED..."

In 1996, Tony Bullimore's yacht capsized as he took part in a single-handed, around-the-world race. People assumed the 57-year-old sailor was dead, but Bullimore managed to survive in an air pocket in his upside-down boat. It was cold, completely dark, and all he had to eat was a bar of chocolate. When a rescue boat knocked on the boat's hull four days later, to their surprise Bullimore swam out to safety.

How to Survive

If people have to abandon a capsized boat, there are several things they should do:
- Send out SOS radio signals to tell people they are in trouble and where they are.
- Grab a life jacket, life raft, and any supplies and emergency items they can carry.
- Get away from the boat before it goes down.

Do or Die

You are on a yacht in the ocean when a huge wave knocks your boat and it starts to capsize. There is no chance of getting it upright. Do you:

a Send out an SOS radio signal?

b Jump straight in the water?

c Stay on the boat as long as you can, until it finally sinks?

STAYING AFLOAT

When a ship goes down or an airplane crashes into the sea, the first and possibly biggest risk to the passengers is death by drowning. Even people who are good swimmers can get into trouble in rough, cold waters. Every year, about 1.2 million people around the world die by drowning, many in the sea, so it is vital to know how to stay afloat in an emergency.

When people fall into water, they sink because of their weight, then they come to the surface again. As they struggle to stay afloat or open their mouth wide to call for help, they may swallow water. It is freezing cold and water will keep hitting them in the face, making it difficult to breathe. It is vital to avoid panicking and thrashing around, because this will make them exhausted quickly.

Life Jackets

The first thing to do when in water is to grab a life jacket or life ring. Both are filled with light materials that float, and they help people float.
If these are not available, people should hold onto anything else that floats, such as a log or **debris** from a boat.

If someone is sinking in the water, holding up their hand can tell rescuers where they are.

Positions for Floating

If there is nothing around to hold onto, people should not panic. The human body has natural **buoyancy** that people can use to keep their face above water. They should lie on their back in the water, with their arms and legs spread out and their back arched. The back of the head will be underwater, but this should keep the face out of the water so they can keep breathing until help arrives.

If people stay calm and float on their back, they have a better chance of survival in the water.

Do or Die

You are on a small boat that is speeding across the sea when you fall overboard into the waves. The boat carries on. Do you:

a Swim as fast as you can after the boat?

b Lie on your back and float until the boat returns for you?

c Thrash around and shout for help?

Life Raft

A life raft greatly increases a person's chances of survival at sea. Life rafts are **inflatable** or solid boats, which larger boats and ships carry in case of emergency. They are launched as soon as a ship is in danger. Life rafts help keep people from drowning or becoming exhausted. They also make shark attacks less likely.

Life rafts usually have space for several people. They are made in bright colors so rescuers can see them from far away. They have a ladder people can use to climb aboard and a nylon roof to shelter people from the elements. People should not swim out to help other victims onto a life raft. They should throw them a line and drag them in.

Do or Die

After the boat you were in sank, you made it onto a life raft. Now another passenger is calling for your help. Do you:

a. Dive in to help him to the raft?

b. Wait until he swims to the raft?

c. Throw a line and pull him in?

Useful Items

Life rafts are usually equipped with first aid kits, fresh drinking water, and distress **flares**, but once inside, it is worth grabbing any useful items that float by. This might include food, water, containers, clothing, and cushions. People should tie the items to the raft so they are not washed away.

"I SURVIVED..."

Steve Callahan loved boats so much that he made his own, and set off to sail it across the Atlantic Ocean. On this voyage, a storm blew up, and a whale or large shark smashed into the boat, creating a hole in the hull. Callahan just had time to get his life raft and supplies ready before abandoning ship. He survived on his rations, fish, and rainwater for 76 days before a ship spotted him.

Without a life raft, someone in 59 degrees Fahrenheit (15 °C) water would be dead in six hours.

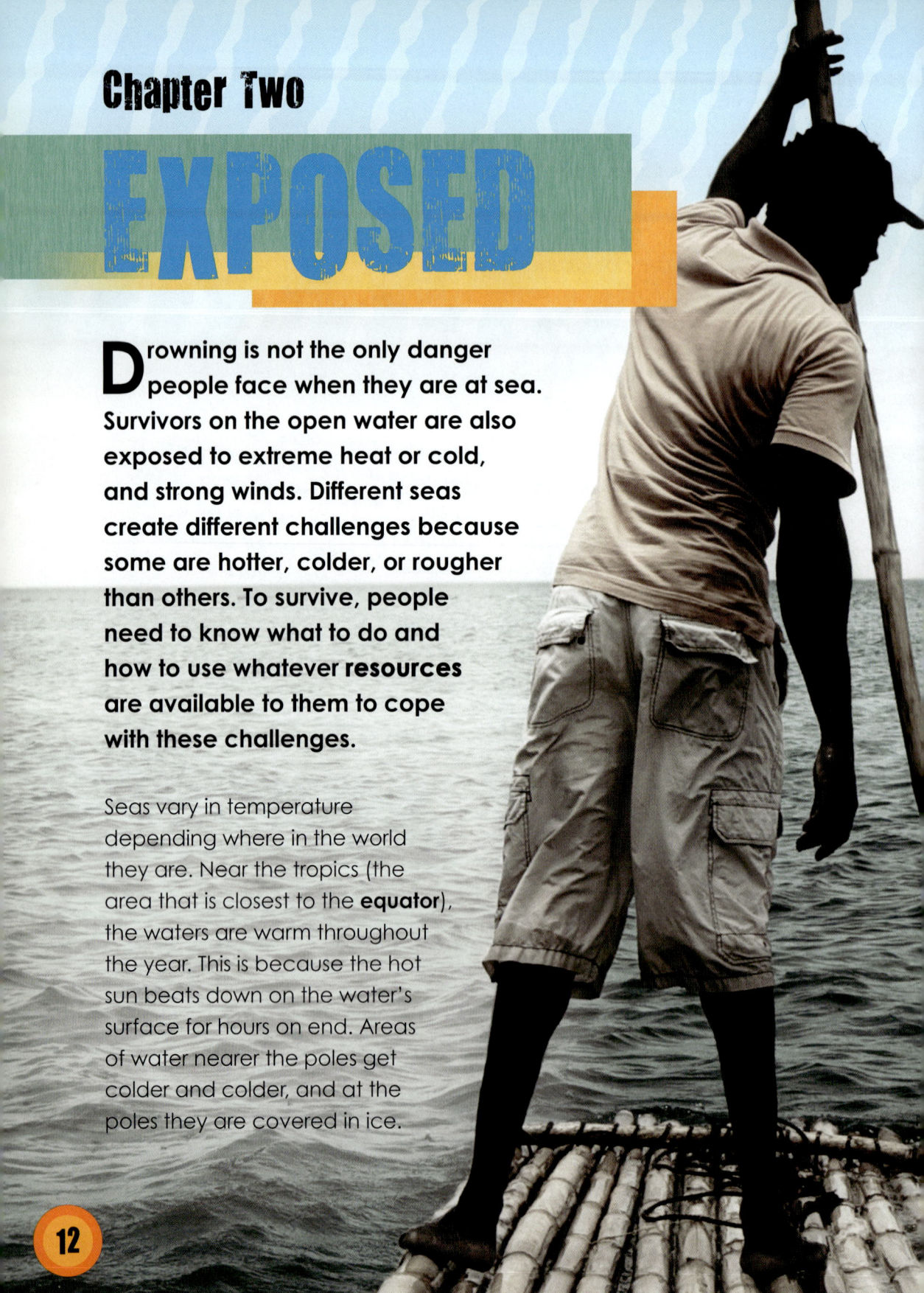

Chapter Two

EXPOSED

Drowning is not the only danger people face when they are at sea. Survivors on the open water are also exposed to extreme heat or cold, and strong winds. Different seas create different challenges because some are hotter, colder, or rougher than others. To survive, people need to know what to do and how to use whatever **resources** are available to them to cope with these challenges.

Seas vary in temperature depending where in the world they are. Near the tropics (the area that is closest to the **equator**), the waters are warm throughout the year. This is because the hot sun beats down on the water's surface for hours on end. Areas of water nearer the poles get colder and colder, and at the poles they are covered in ice.

Cold

Even in warmer waters, cold is a problem, because the body cools six times faster in cold water than it does in air. The **wind-chill factor** makes things worse. The wind blows across the open ocean where there is nothing to block its path. It carries heat away from the body, making people colder.

Keeping Calm

There are a lot of practical things people can do to warm up or cool down if they need to, but it is just as important to remain calm at sea. When people are scared and start to panic, this uses up some of their energy. It also keeps them from thinking clearly. Keeping calm saves energy and helps people think clearly about what they need to do to survive.

On an open raft, people are exposed and have no protection from the sun, wind, cold, and rain.

Do or Die

Your boat sinks and you find yourself adrift on a warm sea in the late afternoon. Do you:

a Relax—you feel warm enough?

b Think calmly about a way to keep warm because you will feel cold soon?

c Swim around in a rush to find floating debris?

CHILLED TO THE BONE

At sea, the cold can be fatal. **Hypothermia** can result if people become too cold. The early signs of hypothermia are when people become confused, cannot control their movements properly, and start to mumble. Eventually, they pass out and then drown. In cold water, dying from hypothermia might occur in a matter of minutes. Even in tropical water, people can die if they are in the water too long without protection.

"I SURVIVED..."

In 2013, a wave upturned the ship Harrison Okene was working on, and the rest of his crew drowned. He made it into an office on the ship, where there was a small pocket of air, before the ship sank to the sea floor. The air kept him alive for more than two days until rescuers arrived. He avoided hypothermia by making a platform with a mattress, which kept him just above the freezing water.

The best way to reduce the risk of hypothermia is to get out of the water as soon possible, into a life raft or onto floating debris. People should try to get dry quickly. If this is impossible, people should wear as many clothes as possible. As well as helping people float, a snug-fitting life jacket can also **insulate** the body from the cold.

HELP

In the sea, movement can increase the loss of body heat. If people cannot get out of the water, they should float in the Heat Escape Lessening Posture (HELP): holding the arms tight against the chest, pressing the thighs together, and raising the knees to protect the groin. This can increase survival rates by nearly 50 percent.

If there is a chance to get out of cold water, people should swim to safety as soon as they can.

Do or Die

You fall overboard into cold water, wearing a shirt and sweatshirt. Do you:

a Take off the sweatshirt to make yourself lighter?

b Stay as you are?

c Grab a life jacket that floats by and put that on, too?

SURVIVING THE SUN

The sun looks pretty shining on the sea's surface. However, when sunlight **reflects** off large, open areas of ocean, it gets very hot for people floating or bobbing along on a boat or life raft. Getting too hot can make people sick and cause heatstroke, a condition in which the body loses its ability to cool down and overheats. It can damage the brain and other **vital organs**.

When sunlight reflects off the ocean, it can also burn the skin. Wearing wet clothing is better than having bare skin as it can help keep people cooler and block the sun. However, the salt in the clothes might rub the skin and make sunburn worse, because salt takes away the skin's natural moisture, and can make skin crack.

Sun Protection

To survive the sun, people should cover their skin, head, and neck, and avoid moving around too much during the day. A sunshade can be made with a broken sail. If people get too hot, they can swim to cool off, but before doing this, they should tie themselves to the boat or raft. They should apply sunblock or use animal fat found in seabirds and other animals as sunblock.

When adrift on a boat in the ocean, people's skin gets burned quickly if it is unprotected.

Eye Safety

Sun reflecting off the sea can damage eyes, so people should wear sunglasses with 100 percent **ultraviolet (UV)** protection. If they do not have sunglasses, they can tie fabric over their eyes and cut two slits for their eyes to see through. This "mask" will allow them to see, but it will cut down contact with the sun's rays.

Do or Die

You are adrift in a tropical sea and the sun is beating down on you in your life raft. Your skin is turning red. Do you:

a Rub saltwater on your skin?

b Put on a wet shirt to help block out the sun?

c Jump into the ocean?

Chapter Three
FOOD AND DRINK

When people set out on an ocean voyage, they take their own supplies of food and water. In order to take enough supplies for a long trip, they should take canned, bottled, or dried foods that will not rot. They should pack more than they think they will need, in case an engine fails or a yacht cannot travel as quickly as it should, because the winds are not as strong as usual.

At sea, people should drink plenty of freshwater, not salty seawater.

Sailors should always carry a lot of drinking water because it is dangerous for people to drink large amounts of seawater. The salt in seawater can make people sick. If they drink too much of it, it can kill them. As the body tries to flush out the extra salt from the seawater, it uses the body's freshwater, which is needed for survival.

Dehydration

If people get into trouble at sea, water is more important than food. A human can survive more than three weeks without food, but only three to four days without water. A lack of water causes dehydration. This is a condition in which the body starts to shut down unless its water is replaced.

Rations

When a life raft is launched, it usually has some supplies of food already on it. The problem for survivors is that they do not know how long it will take to be rescued, so they need to make the food last. That means that before they start eating their supplies, they should figure out how little they can live on every day to make those rations last as long as possible. When planning a trip, it is always better to take more food than needed for the trip in case of disaster.

Even if someone is desperate, they should not drink seawater. After drinking seawater, the body has less water in it than it did before.

Do or Die

You are packing your boat for a long ocean voyage but space is limited. Do you take:

a Just enough food for the voyage?

b Less food than you need because you plan to catch fish?

c More food than you need?

DRINKING WATER

Water, water, everywhere—and not a drop to drink! It is difficult to imagine feeling thirsty in the middle of an ocean surrounded by water, but if people do not know what to do in an emergency when supplies run out, that is exactly what will happen. Using the resources around them, most sea survivors should be able to get enough drinkable water to save their life.

In a boat or life raft, people can make a bowl out of sails, shirts, or any cloth, and collect rainwater. Then they can pour the water into cans, bottles, or containers to make sure they have some for later. It is best to let rain wash salt off a sail first, and then collect water afterward.

"I SURVIVED..."

In 2015, Louis Jordan was missing at sea for 66 days. He was sitting on the overturned hull of his boat 200 miles (320 km) off the coast of North Carolina. He survived by catching fish and drinking rainwater. After collecting rainwater during a shower, he rationed himself to 1 pint (500 mm) of water a day, so he did not run out. He felt thirsty all the time, but survived long enough to be rescued by the crew of a German tanker.

Changing Seawater

Solar stills turn seawater into drinking water. To make a solar still, people should put clear plastic over a bowl of seawater with a cup standing in the middle of the bowl. Then they should put a weight in the middle of the plastic. The sun's heat **evaporates** the seawater. The water vapor that **condenses** on the plastic is pure, and can be drunk after it drips into the cup.

Do or Die

You are stuck on a life raft without any water. Suddenly, there is a heavy rainstorm. Do you:

a Catch as much water as you can in a bowl and drink it all?

b Open your mouth and swallow as much as you can?

c Catch as much water as you can in a bowl, drink some, and save some?

Rain clouds can be a welcome sight for someone lost at sea because people can drink rainwater.

CATCHING FISH

Oceans are an important source of food. Around the world, people get the **protein** they need from the fish that they eat. Protein is a substance that the body needs to grow, develop, and repair itself properly. Fish might be easier to catch than people think. Small fish often gather beneath a boat or life raft, perhaps because they feel sheltered there, **and sometimes flying fish jump right onto a boat.**

Some fish have spikes and can be dangerous, but, luckily, in the open ocean, most fish are safe to eat. Fish are not only a good source of food, they also contain water. There is liquid in their flesh, eyes, and backbone. To get to these liquids, survivors need to cut open the fish, break the backbone, and suck out the juices.

In the ocean, fish often swim in groups called shoals. This can make them easier to catch.

It is easier to catch fish if survivors have or can make a net.

Making a Net

It is very difficult to catch fish by hand, so people can use cloth to make a net. They should hold it in the water and pull it up quickly when fish pass by. They can also bend wire into a hook, and tie it to string with something shiny to attract fish. After catching a fish, people can use the dead fish's insides as bait to catch more fish on the hook.

Keeping Fish Fresh

Fish will rot quickly after they are pulled from the ocean. To make them last, people can cut strips of fish meat and hang them in the sun to dry. These dried snacks will last much longer, and they will still provide the body with nourishment.

Do or Die

You are adrift at sea on a raft and are managing to catch enough rainwater to drink, but you need to catch some fish for food. Do you:

a Bend wire into a hook, and attach something shiny or colorful to it?

b Bend wire into a hook and dangle it over the side?

c Hold your hands underwater and wait to grab a passing fish?

OTHER FOODS

Fish are not the only food in the ocean that people can eat. There are no plants, but seaweed is an algae that can be eaten. People should eat only living seaweed. They can eat it raw, fried, or broiled like a vegetable. Seaweed can be tough and it is salty, so it should be eaten only when people have plenty of drinking water.

Out at sea, most seabirds are safe to catch and eat, and they can be eaten raw or cooked. Many seabirds float on the water's surface, looking out for fish to catch to eat. If they land close to a boat, people can catch the birds. Sometimes, birds land on a raft or boat, making them even easier to catch.

Sea turtles are an **endangered species**, but as a last resort, some survivors have been forced to eat one or two in order to stay alive.

Catching Turtles

Ideally, people avoid eating sea turtles because they are an endangered species, but if the situation is desperate, these animals can provide food and water. Turtles are also fairly easy to catch because they have to come to the water's surface every few minutes to breathe.

"I SURVIVED..."

In 2012, José Alvarenga set out from a fishing village on the Mexican coast with a fellow fisherman. Bad weather blew the men into the ocean. Alvarenga's friend died about a month later, after getting sick. Alvarenga claims he survived for 13 months by eating fish, birds, and turtles, and by drinking turtle blood and rainwater.

Do or Die

You are lost at sea for a week and hungry. You catch a lot of fish and a sea turtle in a net. Do you:

a Eat both?

b Eat the turtle?

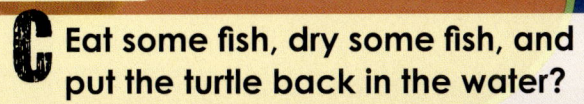

c Eat some fish, dry some fish, and put the turtle back in the water?

Chapter Four

UNDER ATTACK!

The sea is full of living creatures, and some of them can be dangerous and deadly to humans. Animals that live in oceans have special **adaptations** to help them survive there. For example, fish and other animals that live underwater all the time have **gills** to help them breathe air from the water. Animals, such as seals and dolphins, come to the surface to breathe air.

To get the water they need, fish drink the salty seawater and then get rid of it through their gills. Other animals such as seals and whales get the water they need from the animals they eat. The adaptations animals have to help them catch **prey** or escape predators is often what makes them dangerous to humans.

Lionfish do not attack people but give a nasty sting from their spines if someone touches them.

Stingers and Venom

Lionfish are beautiful to look at but people should never try to touch them. They can give a very painful sting with some powerful **venom**. Sea snake venom is also dangerous to people if a snake bites, although sea snakes usually keep out of people's way.

Stingrays

A stingray's tail can whip back and deliver a fatal sting if it feels under threat. When people are in the sea, or plan to get into the sea from a boat or raft, they need to take care. They should always check the water first and keep looking around. Most stingray attacks happen when divers and swimmers accidentally step on them, so people should watch where they walk.

Most sea snakes live underwater and only come up for air. Sea snakes are very poisonous.

Do or Die

You are swimming when you spot a lionfish ahead. You want to show friends back on the boat what you saw. Do you:

a Grab the fish to take it back to the boat?

b Swim away and avoid it?

c Follow the lionfish as it swims?

SHARKS

Sharks are one of the deadliest predators in the sea. They do not usually hunt people as prey. Sharks usually hunt seals, and most attack humans only because their dark shape looks seal-like when seen from deep water below. Once a shark realizes the thing it is biting into is not a juicy fat seal, it usually (but not always…) lets go. A shark's bite can be fatal.

Sharks are successful predators because they have a **streamlined** shape to move swiftly through the water. A large, powerful tails propels them forward fast. They shoot up from under the water and slam into seals floating near the surface, biting into them with a set of very sharp teeth. Great white sharks bite into their prey with a mouthful of 300 jagged teeth.

"I SURVIVED…"

In 1953, Rodney Fox was spear-fishing when a great white shark grabbed him and dragged him into the water. Fox poked the shark's eyes until the shark released him, but then the shark bit into him again. This time, Fox thrust his arm down the throat of the beast and the shark let him go. Then, the shark attacked for a third time, dragging Fox along the ocean floor until he nearly drowned. Suddenly, the shark let him go, and Fox made it to a nearby boat, badly injured but alive.

Self-defense

Sharks are attracted to movement, so people should avoid thrashing around. They should instead swim slowly away. Sharks smell blood, so people should keep injured parts out of water or strapped up. If a shark approaches, people should hit its eyes and gills with a stick, knife, or even an arm, to chase it away.

> Great white sharks shoot up suddenly from deep, dark water to surprise victims at the surface.

Do or Die

You are floating in the sea when you glimpse a shark's fin a little way away. Your boat is nearby. Do you:

a. Swim as fast as you can to safety?
b. Swim gently and slowly to the boat?
c. Get ready to punch the shark?

JELLYFISH

Some kinds of jellyfish rank among the most dangerous animals in the sea because they have such deadly stings. Jellyfish are not fish but are named for their squishy, jelly-like body. Some jellyfish can hurt people because they have millions of very small stinging parts in their **tentacles**. They inject stings into their prey to capture it. If people are stung by the tentacles, the poison goes through their skin, too.

Most jellyfish float along on the ocean currents, waiting for food to pass by. They eat whatever their long tentacles can catch, including small fish, eggs, and **larvae** of sea creatures. Larger types of jellyfish eat **crustaceans** and even other jellyfish. Some, like the Australian box jellyfish, chase their prey.

Avoiding a Sting

To avoid a jellyfish sting, people should not go into water where jellyfish are known to be. When swimming in an area, they should make sure they know what types of jellyfish might be around. Wearing protective clothing such as a long wet suit, gloves, and boots will protect the skin when swimming. People must not pick up dead jellyfish because jellyfish tentacles can still sting when the creature is dead.

> There are more than 200 different species of jellyfish. Some are tiny, but others are bigger than a human!

Do or Die

You are planning to go snorkeling out at sea in an area where they might be jellyfish. Do you wear:

a A long wet suit, gloves, and boots?

b Just your swimsuit?

c Goggles so you can see better?

Treating a Sting

People should carry a basic first aid kit with them at sea. This should include **antihistamine** medicine, which will reduce the itching and mild pain caused by a jellyfish sting. If the symptoms are bad, such as severe pain, swelling, or difficulty breathing, then people should see a doctor immediately.

"I SURVIVED..."

When Australian schoolgirl Rachael Shardlow was 10 years old, she was stung on the legs by a box jellyfish, the world's most venomous animal. Within moments, she could not see or breathe, and she fell unconscious. Box jellyfish victims usually die within three minutes of being stung. Amazingly, Rachael survived and although she spent six weeks in a coma in the hospital and had badly scarred legs, she lived to tell the tale!

PIRATES!

Sea creatures, such as sharks and jellyfish, are not the only dangerous things at sea. Modern-day pirates are just as terrifying as the pirates of the past. These criminals board boats either in port or out at sea, to steal the money and valuables inside. Sometimes, they steal the boat, too. They also kidnap people from their boats and hold them for **ransom**, until their families pay large sums of money to get them back safely.

The best way to avoid pirates is to stay away from the waters where they operate. Before setting off on an ocean voyage, people should find out where piracy and other criminal activities are happening. Then they can plan routes to avoid those areas or perhaps plan to pass through them at the same time as other ships, because there is safety in numbers.

"I SURVIVED..."

While sailing his sailing ship between Panama and Hawaii, Matt Bracken realized a large steel ship was following him. He knew something was wrong, so he took out a black spray-painted plywood gun, which looked large and threatening. When the pirates saw the weapon through their binoculars they decided it was not worth the risk of attacking Bracken, and sped away. It was a narrow escape.

Do or Die

You are planning a long ocean voyage on a yacht with a friend. When planning your route, do you:

a Choose a route to see whales?

b Avoid areas pirates are known to frequent?

c Choose a route to see deserted islands?

One way to avoid a pirate attack is to keep a lookout for any suspicious boats while in dangerous waters.

Modern-day pirates sometimes stop and board large, luxury yachts like this one, to steal valuables.

Keeping Safe

If the worst happens and pirates board a ship, the safest tactic is for people on board not to argue or fight with the thieves. They should let the pirates take what they want, including the boat if necessary. Objects can be replaced and it is better not to risk making the pirates angry.

33

Chapter Five

NAVIGATION

People who have sent a **Mayday** message or who have crash-landed in a plane should stay where they are, so a rescue party can find them. In a life raft, people may have no choice but to float on the ocean current. Even if people can row or paddle away, it is difficult to know which way to go in the middle of an ocean with no landmarks or islands in view.

To help them find their way, sailors need equipment such as a **compass** and **global positioning system (GPS)** devices. A compass has a needle that always points north, so people can figure out the direction in which to travel. GPS units use **satellite** links to pinpoint where people are, to help them decide where they need to go.

If sailors keep track of where they are on a sea chart, they will have a better idea of where to go if there is an emergency.

Tides and Currents

Sailors also need to learn about tides and currents as both can affect in which direction a boat travels. They should carry charts that show ports they can use in an emergency, and features that help with **navigation**, such as lighthouses and small islands.

34

Seeing Stars

If people do not have the right equipment, they can use the sun and stars to navigate. The sun can help with directions because it rises in the east and sets in the west. If people know which star is the North Star in the night sky they can find their way, too. If they follow the North Star to the nearest point on the horizon, this shows the direction north.

If someone is lost at sea, using the stars to navigate can help them find their way again.

Do or Die

You have crash-landed in the sea, but you are in a lifeboat that has an engine. Do you:

a Start the engine and head off in one direction?

b Wait until night and use the stars to navigate?

c Stay where you are and wait for rescue?

RISKY LANDINGS

As people navigate across the ocean, they should keep a lookout for any signs of land. Seabirds can help people locate islands, because they tend to fly out to sea to hunt for fish in the daytime. Then, in the evening, they head back toward land. Unfortunately, even if people reach an island, there is a danger that they will be injured or killed as they try to land.

Ocean winds can whip up high waves that can crash against coasts. As the water gets shallower near a shore, waves become taller. These high waves can tip rafts over or engulf swimmers. There can also be dangerous riptides. These are areas of rough water in the sea that can be caused by sudden changes in depth.

Imagine the relief it must be to spot land after being lost at sea, drifting on a life raft.

Coral Reefs

People can also get hurt by rough coral reefs or jagged rocks along a shoreline. Coral reefs are rocklike structures built by millions of tiny animals called polyps. Coral reefs can create a barrier that protects shorelines from rough waves, but they can also rip open the side of a boat.

Coral reefs often grow near the coastline around islands.

Play It Safe

Even if it is a huge relief when people find an island after days lost at sea, they must take care. If the coast they see is full of jagged rocks and high waves, they should circle the island to find a better landing spot. If the whole island is too rough to land on, they should travel on to find one with a sandy shore and gentle waves.

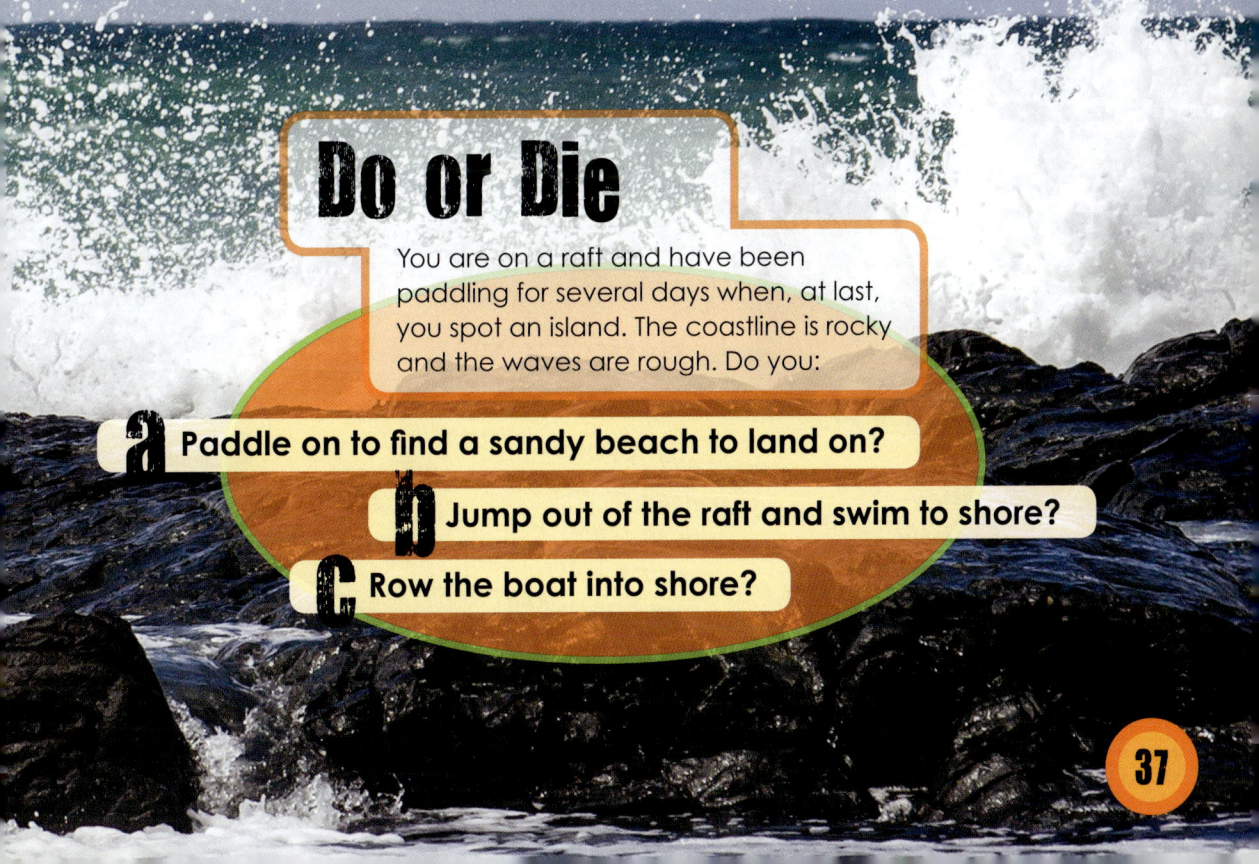

Do or Die

You are on a raft and have been paddling for several days when, at last, you spot an island. The coastline is rocky and the waves are rough. Do you:

a Paddle on to find a sandy beach to land on?

b Jump out of the raft and swim to shore?

c Row the boat into shore?

STRANDED!

If people make it to an island, there is a good chance they will be able to survive for a long time. Many islands have streams that supply freshwater to drink, and plants and animals that people can eat. If there are no streams, people can crack open coconuts and drink the watery milk inside. Coconuts float across the sea and take root and grow on many island shores.

The first job on an island is to make a shelter. At night, clouds (that have formed from the huge amounts of water that evaporate from the ocean during the day) release their water as rain. The rain will make people feel very cold, even on a warm island. People can build shelters from old sails or wood, with a roof of branches and leaves.

"I SURVIVED..."

Surviving alone on a desert island is possible. Juana Maria, who was the last surviving member of her tribe, lived alone on San Nicolas Island for 18 years. She ate fish and dried seal meat, lived in a hut partly made from whale bones, and wore clothes made of cormorant skins. She was strong and healthy when rescued in 1853, but she died just seven weeks later.

Animal Dangers

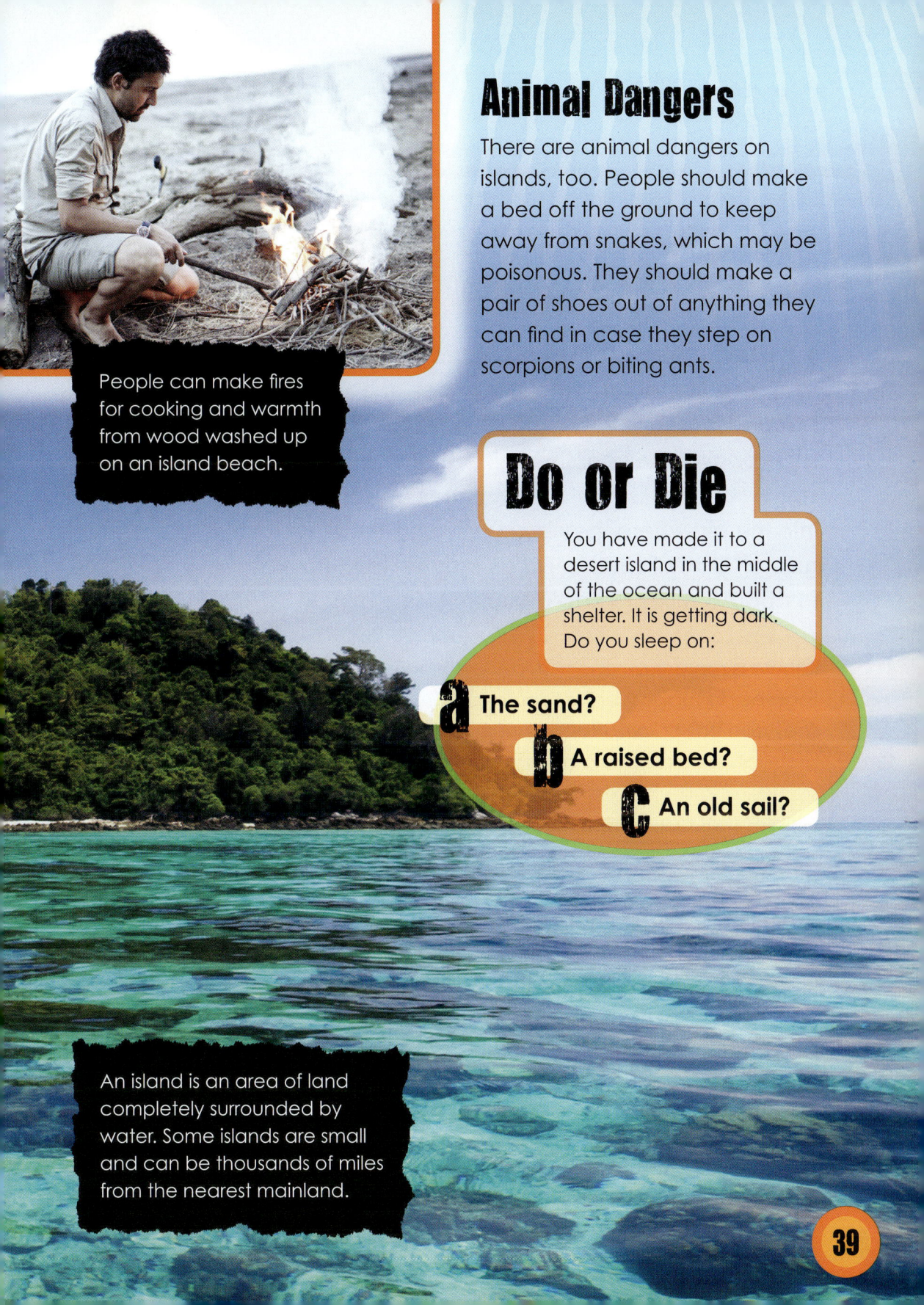

There are animal dangers on islands, too. People should make a bed off the ground to keep away from snakes, which may be poisonous. They should make a pair of shoes out of anything they can find in case they step on scorpions or biting ants.

People can make fires for cooking and warmth from wood washed up on an island beach.

Do or Die

You have made it to a desert island in the middle of the ocean and built a shelter. It is getting dark. Do you sleep on:

a The sand?

b A raised bed?

c An old sail?

An island is an area of land completely surrounded by water. Some islands are small and can be thousands of miles from the nearest mainland.

Chapter Six

RESCUE!

Whether stranded on an island, a boat, or a life raft, people's chances of being rescued increase if they have ways to signal ships or airplanes passing by. The best way to signal rescuers is with a flare. Flares can be shot into the air, where they burn very brightly or give off a lot of smoke. Flares can be seen up to about 3 miles (5 km) away for a few minutes.

If there is more than one raft, people can join rafts together to make them easier to spot from the sky. They can trail colored fabric behind a boat or raft. Lifeboats should have a horn to give off loud honking sounds, and life jackets are usually equipped with whistles that can be blown to attract attention.

Sending Signals

On an island, people can make fires. Fires are also a good way to send signals after dark. Ideally people should build three fires in a row, because this is an international distress signal. One fire on its own might just look like people are having a beach party.

Fires are a good way to signal for help at night.

At Night

To send signals from the sea at night, people could turn a flashlight on and off to attract attention from boats or aircraft. During the daytime, they could reflect sunlight off a mirror to send signals. If someone is in the water, they could wave their hands slowly at people in nearby boats. This signal says: "I am in distress, help me!"

Flares are a clear signal that someone needs help and tells rescuers where they are.

Do or Die

You are lost at sea on a small raft and have one flare left. You hear a plane in the distance. Do you:

a Set off the flare immediately?

b Wait until the plane is in view and then set off the flare?

c Save the flare because you are pretty sure the plane will see you?

41

BE PREPARED

The seas and oceans of the world are exciting, wild places to explore. When people understand the risks and prepare for ocean trips properly, they should be safe, too. Of course, accidents can happen, the weather can change and whip up dangerous, freak waves, and equipment can fail. Even then, people can survive if they keep calm. Remaining calm helps people think clearly and helps them get through the ordeal alive.

Being confident that they know what to do in an emergency and the ability to keep calm helps keep people safe at sea.

Plan Ahead

Before setting off, people should plan their route carefully, check weather forecasts, and let others know exactly where they plan to be and when. Rescuers will then know where to go if people get into trouble at sea. They should learn how to make minor repairs to their boat and have the equipment they might need to do so. They should take navigation equipment, but also learn how to navigate using nature.

Packing Supplies

Having the right equipment can save lives. People should pack ample food and water supplies, and make sure they have life jackets, lifeboats, and flares. They should pack a first aid kit and items such as flashlights, mirrors, and knives, which can make the difference between life and death in an emergency.

A life jacket keeps the wearer safe at sea.

Do or Die

You are on an ocean trip on a sailboat with friends when one friend says she would like to stop at an island for a few days. Do you:

a Stop on the island for a few days?

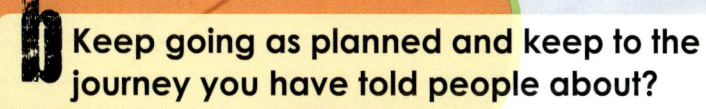

b Keep going as planned and keep to the journey you have told people about?

c Keep going but then stop at another island anyway?

ANSWERS

Would you survive if you were on your own and stranded in the sea? Check your answers against these correct ones to see if you know how to survive.

Pages 6–7
Answer: A

It's best to stay calm and call for help. You should get useful supplies before leaving the boat, but you should not stay on board too long or you may go down with your ship.

Pages 8–9
Answer: B

If you shout and splash, you may swallow too much water and drown. If you swim too hard, you may get exhausted and drown. Try to stay afloat until people realize you are missing and come back.

Pages 10–11
Answer: C

People may not be able to make it to the raft and you should not swim to them because you could drown, too. Using a line to pull them in is much safer.

Pages 12–13
Answer: B

Do not panic, but do not relax so much that you forget to make a plan to cope with the elements. Even in a warm place, you will get cold in water, so take time to think about how to cope.

Pages 14–15
Answer: C

Layers will trap warmth from your body and help keep you from getting colder faster. A life jacket will provide a layer of warmth against the cold.

Pages 16–17
Answer: B

Saltwater will make sunburn worse, so splashing with water or jumping into the ocean should be avoided. Putting on a wet shirt will help block out some of the sun's rays.

Pages 18–19
Answer: C

Always take more food than you need in case you are delayed. It is better to have food supplies with you than to rely on catching fish.

Pages 20–21
Answer: C

You never know when it will rain again, so it is a good idea to collect as much rainwater as you possibly can. Try to store some water in containers to save for later.

Pages 22–23
Answer: A
Using something shiny or colorful on a hook helps attract a fish to the hook, because the fish thinks it is prey glistening in the water.

Pages 24–25
Answer: C
Eat some fish, dry some for later, and throw the sea turtle back in the sea. The sea turtle is an endangered species and you should try to avoid eating it if you can.

Pages 26–27
Answer: B
Lionfish will not chase you, but they will sting if you try to touch them. It is best to stay away from them.

Pages 28–29
Answer: B
Swimming slowly back to safety is your best chance. If you thrash around, the shark will spot you. It is not worth waiting for a shark to attack if there is a chance you could get out of the water instead.

Pages 30–31
Answer: A
Do not take chances where they may be jellyfish. Cover skin with a protective layer that stings cannot get through.

Pages 32–33
Answer: B
The best way to avoid being taken hostage by pirates or having all your belongings and your ship stolen is to stay out of waters where pirate attacks happen. It is not worth taking any risks.

Pages 34–35
Answer: C
Do not leave the crash site because airplanes follow set routes and rescuers will be on their way. If you leave the site, you may be too far from land to survive, and you could get lost.

Pages 36–37
Answer: A
It is just as dangerous to swim as to row ashore in a boat if the coastline is rocky and rough. It is better to be safe than sorry, and keep rowing until you find a safe beach to land on.

Pages 38–39
Answer: B
It is better to sleep on a bed that is raised off the ground away from scorpions and snakes that scuttle and slither over the ground. Many scorpions and snakes can deliver painful stings or bites.

Pages 40–41
Answer: B
Do not set off a flare too early because flares burn for only a few minutes. Always use a flare because, from the sky, one person on a raft is easy to miss.

Pages 42–43
Answer: B
Unless you can notify people who are expecting you to be at a certain place at a certain time, you should keep to a planned route. If you are late for your next stop, they may send out rescue parties.

GLOSSARY

adaptations features that help an animal or plant survive in its habitat
antihistamine a medicine used to treat the body's reactions to something like a sting or bite
buoyancy the ability to float
capsize to turn over in the water
compass a device with a magnetized pointer that shows the direction of north
condenses turns from a gas into a liquid (for example, from water vapor into water)
crustaceans animals (such as a crab) that have several pairs of legs and a body made up of sections that are covered by a hard outer shell
debris pieces left over after something has been destroyed
endangered species a type of animal that soon may no longer exist
equator an imaginary line around the middle of Earth, where it is hottest
evaporates turns from liquid into a gas
flare a device that can send up a flash of light or smoke to send a signal
friction the force that occurs when two surfaces slide against each other
gills body parts that allow fish to breathe underwater
global positioning system (GPS) a system that helps people find their location on a map
hypothermia a condition in which the body gets too cold to function
inflatable blown up with air
insulate to keep heat or cold from moving from one place to another

larvae the young, often wormlike form of some animals
Mayday an radio-telephone signal word used as a distress call
navigation finding one's way around
predators animals that hunt and eat other animals
prey an animal that is hunted and eaten by other animals
protein a substance found in food that people need to survive
ransom money paid to kidnappers to ensure a captive's release
rations particular amounts of food that are given to one person or animal for one day
reflects throws or bends back light or sound
resources things that provide something useful
satellite an electronic device high in space that moves around Earth
solar stills small devices that convert saltwater into drinkable water using the sun
streamlined a long, thin torpedo shape that moves easily through water
tentacles the long, flexible arms of an animal such as an octopus or jellyfish
ultraviolet (UV) invisible rays given off by the sun that can harm human skin and eyes
venom a poison made by some animals
vital organs parts of the body people need to stay alive
wind-chill factor the way it feels colder when the wind blows hard

FOR MORE INFORMATION

Books

Rizzo, Johnna. *Ocean Animals: Who's Who in the Deep Blue*. Washington, D.C.: National Geographic Children's Books, 2016.

Sharks and Other Deadly Ocean Creatures Visual Encyclopedia. New York, NY: Dorling Kindersley, 2016.

Rice, William. *Survival Ocean*. Huntington Beach, CA: Teacher Created Materials, 2013.

Spilsbury, Louise and Richard. *Pacific Ocean* (Young Explorer: Oceans of the World). North Mankato, MN: Raintree, 2016.

Websites

Click on one of the links in this NASA Ocean menu to find out more about oceans, play games, and more at:
http://climatekids.nasa.gov/menu/ocean

Read lots of amazing facts about the ocean at:
http://ocean.nationalgeographic.com/ocean

Click on the "For students" section of this National Ocean and Atmospheric Administration (NOAA) website for fascinating information about oceans and seas:
http://oceanservice.noaa.gov/education

Publisher's note to educators and parents: Our editors have carefully reviewed these websites to ensure that they are suitable for students. Many websites change frequently, however, and we cannot guarantee that a site's future contents will continue to meet our high standards of quality and educational value. Be advised that students should be closely supervised whenever they access the Internet.

INDEX

airplanes 5, 8, 34, 40, 41
Atlantic Ocean 11

buoyancy 9

capsized 6–7
compasses 34
coral reefs 37
crustaceans 30
currents 30, 34

dehydration 18
drinking water 4, 11, 18, 20–21, 24
drowning 8, 10, 12

eye safety 17

fires 5, 39, 40
fish 11, 19, 20, 22–23, 24, 25, 26, 30, 36, 38
flares 11, 40, 41, 43
food 4, 11, 18–19, 22, 23, 24–25, 30, 43

global positioning systems (GPS) 34

Hawaii 32
Heat Escape Lessening Position (HELP) 15
heatstroke 16
hypothermia 14, 15

islands 33, 34, 36, 37, 38, 39, 40, 43

jellyfish 30–31, 32

life jackets 7, 8, 15, 40, 43
life ring 8
lionfish 26, 27

Mayday 34

navigation 34, 43
North Carolina 20

Panama 32
pirates 32–33
predators 4, 26, 28

rafts 5, 7, 10–11, 13, 15, 16, 17, 19, 20, 21, 22, 23, 24, 27, 34, 36, 37, 40, 41
rain 13, 20, 21, 38
rations 11, 19
rescuers 5, 8, 10, 14, 40, 41, 43

sea snakes 26, 27
sea turtles 24, 25
seabirds 24
seals 26, 28, 38
seawater 18, 19, 21, 26
sharks 10, 11, 28–29
shelter 10, 38, 39
signals 5, 7, 40, 41
solar stills 21
SOS radio signal 7
stars 35
stingrays 27
sun protection 16
sunburn 16

tides 34
tropics 12

venom 26

waves 4, 6, 7, 9, 14, 36, 37, 42
wind-chill factor 13
winds 4, 6, 12, 13, 18, 36

48